Tales

of a

Gravedigger

By

Ian Shipley

Grosvenor House
Publishing Limited

This book is published by
Grosvenor House Publishing Ltd
Link House
140 The Broadway, Tolworth, Surrey, KT6 7HT.
www.grosvenorhousepublishing.co.uk

A CIP record for this book
is available from the British Library

ISBN 978-1-83975-691-7

Dedication

Alison Shipley-Whitehead
To All My Family

With thanks to:
Viv Whitehead
Boz Mugabe (Artwork)

Contents

CHAPTER 1

Newark Cemetery

The old-timers often referred to Newark Cemetery as the "London Road Guest House", where everyone checks in but very few leave.

In 1856 the parish churchyard of St Mary Magdalene, in the centre of Newark-on-Trent, ceased to be used for burials when it was announced that the churchyard was full to capacity. A national rise in the UK population had resulted in many churchyards simply running out of space. The Burial Act of 1853 enabled parishes and boroughs to administer their own cemeteries, electing their own Burial Boards to manage them.

In August 1854, 200 handbills were printed and distributed around the neighbourhood of Newark. Wanted was at least five acres of land suitable for a burial ground. Tenders were received and studied by the Reverend J. Waterworth.

Various sites were offered, including land between Winthorpe Road and Lincoln Road, Beacon Hill and Sconce Hills. By March 1855 the Burial Board had purchased nine acres of land from the Earl of Winchelsea. The land was on the Balderton Road.

In August 1855 the Burial Board invited designs for the layout of the new burial ground. By mid-September a number of designs had been received. They were made available for public inspection, and finally the board agreed that Messrs Bellamy and Hardy of Lincoln be awarded the £10 premium (first prize).

The tender to complete the work was won by George Whitworth of Newark. The work included two chapels joined by a tower and spire, a lodge, a wall to divide the front ground from the burial ground, a front fence and entrance gate, fencing, roads, planting and drainage and a wooden fence on two sides and one end, all in accordance with Bellamy and Hardy's plans.

The work began in January 1856. Initially, all work was due to be completed by March, but that deadline was impossible to meet. After a second delay, a further extension was granted until the end of October 1856.

On Thursday, 30 October 1856, the Church of England section of the new cemetery was consecrated by the Bishop of Lincoln. Soon after the ceremony the first interment took place. The burial was of a three-year-old child named Charles John Nicholson. The cause of death was recorded as hydrocephalus, a condition in which fluid accumulates in the brain.

Six days later the new cemetery had its second burial. Another child, by the name of Edward Ball, aged 11.

He was the son of a grocer. The cause of death was recorded as "accidentally killed by a railway train". Interestingly enough, out of the first 28 interments in Newark only three were in purchased plots; the rest were "Class C's".

"Class C'" registered graves are common graves (paupers' plots). These graves can contain any number of unrelated people. I was aware that some of these were dug to 9ft, (four interments). What I later discovered was that the water table was so low that graves could be dug up to 12-15 feet deep. I don't believe any were; besides, that's a frightening depth to dig to.

Looking through the first registered book of burials, which is now kept at the town hall, I found an interesting discrepancy. In the records it is recorded that John Lane, a schoolmaster, had died on the 11 November 1856 and was buried on the 14th. Oddly, on his headstone, which can be found in the old section of the cemetery, it reads that John Lane departed from this life on the 16 November 1856. So, does this mean that he was buried before he died?

On 7 January 1857 the Burial Board appointed William Newton as registrar and Gilbert Hawkesley as groundskeeper and gravedigger.

The first resident sexton at Newark cemetery was a man called Samuel Rockley. His term in office lasted some nine years until his own death, aged 59, on 26 June 1866 (his headstone can be found in the cemetery).

I have only found reference to one other known sexton, who was in office at the turn of the century, and that was of a Mr F.H. Taylor (1901). His name can be found on the base of the cemetery's ornamental sundial.

A sexton is the traditional name for the caretaker of a churchyard or cemetery. His duties would normally include bell-ringing, gravedigging, record-keeping and any other general maintenance". Very often he would live on-site, and in times gone by he would have been a well-respected pillar of the community.

The cemetery has been extended three times. The first was in 1877, then again in 1901 and again in 1984. The cemetery's fourth extension, though as yet not in use, was landscaped and prepared in 2001.

The chapel, now a grade II listed building, was closed for public use in the mid-1980s. I can recall it being used for the occasional funeral, though it was mostly used as a place for quiet contemplation. It also housed the cemetery's *Book of Remembrance*. By the mid-1980s repeated vandalism resulted in the chapel's closure. From that point on it has been used a storeroom. In recent years there has been talk of reopening it as a museum, though nothing has come of this.

The original cemetery lodge, built in 1856, stood where the main car park off London Road is today, but by 1863 it was in such a poor state that the Burial Board decided to demolish it and rebuild another at a cost of £200. The new lodge was built on the same site as before by contractors Hancock and Snell. This building was demolished in the early 1970s, and a new one, which stands today, was built in 1973.

Other interesting cemetery features include a Second World War air-raid shelter, which can still be found in the cemetery grounds. It stands on the corner, where Elm Avenue joins London Road. It was once the workmen's mess, though for many years now it too has been used as a store.

There was at one time an apple orchard, though this area has now become part of someone's back garden. The original gateway can still be found. It was built into the boundary wall, which divides back gardens from the cemetery, running along the back of Bromley Avenue. I recall that in my early years this area was cut and maintained by cemetery workmen. I seem to think that over time this piece of land may have been forgotten about. I was told by the cemetery's old-timers that the orchard was originally cared for by nuns whose convent was once the Old Magnus Building (now part of Magnus School).

Also hidden away in the same corner as the orchard, near to where the school playing field is today, was the old brick-built morgue building. This too belonged to the nuns; it was where the nuns cared and prayed for their own dead until burial. This building was demolished in 1981.

There was once an old donkey stable that backed onto the "Old Gravedigger's Cottage". This too was a workman's hut, and for many years it was also home to a real live, working donkey. What a sight that would have been! This building was later pulled down after a fire destroyed it.

If you enter the cemetery via the gate at Bromley Avenue and turn right and follow the side path for about 250 yards, you will find among the newer headstones standing on the path side two old-style, sandstone memorials. I am told that there used to be a farm near to where the graves are positioned: the Richardson's farm. Apparently, after the cemetery was extended, in 1901, the family asked if they could have the two family graves in sight of the farmhouse window. Hence, the reason they are where they are today!

The Polish War Graves section, with approximately 500 graves, is one of the biggest in the country and is still regularly visited. This section is the resting place for mostly Polish airmen who died between 1939 and 1945. It was also the resting place of the Polish wartime leader, Wladyslaw Sikorski, who was buried in Newark on Friday, 16 July 1943. For 50 years his body remained here until it was finally exhumed and returned to Poland in 1993.

Tommy Tate was the superintendent at Newark cemetery from 1961–81. He had a passion for the war graves section and the way in which it was kept. He was proud to have won two silver medals for its upkeep, though deep down he always wanted to win the gold!

The first Garden of Remembrance section opened for use in 1967. Situated on the right-hand side of the main drive as you come in from the London Road end, it was the first area dedicated for the burial of ashes and cremated remains. The first interment was on 23 August 1967. It was eventually closed to new burials in 1993. At the same time a new area was opened on the opposite side. The first burial here was on 18 October 1993. This too is now full, though a further extension was opened on 21 January 2005.

Newark cemetery is now approaching its 150th year of use. I've often thought how good it would be to be able to go back in time. It would be great to see how it looked back then—to watch them grave dig, to see them fix those large memorials, to witness an old-style funeral. Fascinating. An eye opener for sure.

CHAPTER 2

In at the Deep End

My career as a gravedigger began at Newark Cemetery on 11 May 1982. My first dig was a new 6ft 6in double grave, which just happened to be in what was at that time the hardest part of the cemetery. It was known as the infamous "B row". I remember it well. It was only my second day, and my work colleague, Ted, had already told me that this would either make or break me. Well, I guess that if I was going to start anywhere, then this was indeed the place to begin.

B row – This line of graves, which ran parallel to the main drive, began in front of the Polish War Graves, near to the first lime tree, and stretched for some 70 plots. At the time it was virtually the last piece of virgin ground on this section. Digging here was renowned for being a tough manual challenge. It was tediously slow going; tree roots were a real problem, with some being as thick as your thigh. Soil-wise, once past the thin layer of topsoil, you'd be into white sand. This was so fine, that it was like trying to shovel out water. At three feet it turned into a well-compacted mixture of red clay and gravel, dry and hard to shift. From this point on it was all pick work.

For my first dig I was to team up with an old boy called Edmund Scott. He was a quiet, rough-looking, well-experienced, white-haired gent who could chain-smoke a packet of Park Drive quicker than you could eat your snap. He was true old school, last of the traditional old-timers, one of those "there's always tomorrow" types—a nice bloke, and not a truer word said.

I was soon to find that digging freehand while trying to keep both sides of the coffin-shaped hole flush and straight was not as easy as it looked. I don't care what anyone says, there is an art to it! I also found twisting and turning in such a confined space, which at best could be only two feet wide at the shoulders, tapering down to a mere 15 inches at the foot, to be nothing but awkward, never mind swinging a pick.

I'm not ashamed to say that I found it tough going. I recall that I ached for days afterwards, as I had used and discovered muscles that I never knew I had. Ted was quick to point out that the best remedy was to simply "dig another". It may sound daft, but he was right.

My first attempt at gravedigging had been an eye-opener. It had been harder than I had imagined, but I had not been put off, and the sense of achievement I felt was great.

I was somewhat worried as to whether the coffin would go in, as once the grave was dressed, it did look small. First dig nerves, though I need not have worried, as all went well. I had dug my first grave! One day I may get the opportunity to reopen this dig and so view my initial handiwork in full.

CHAPTER 3

The Knowledge

It did not take me long to realize that the job was about much more than just digging a hole. It was not as simple as it looked, and there was a lot to learn. And yes, there is an art to it. It was another old-timer, Ted Sumner, who was to teach me all that I needed to know.

Firstly, I was amazed to discover just how many types of graves there could be. New graves, which were usually family plots, began at 4ft 6in deep (single), then increased in size: 6ft 6in (double), 6ft 6in plus a tiny bit out at the bottom (double plus small child), 7ft 6in (treble) and 7ft 6in plus a tiny bit out of the bottom (treble plus child).

Of course, many of these graves would at some point have to be reopened. There were also "Class C" type graves. These were common unmarked graves which were often referred to as "paupers' plots". As mentioned previously, some of these were originally dug to a depth of nine feet (four burials). Finally, there were single child graves and the occasional brick-built vault.

So why is a double grave dug to 6ft 6in?

All cemeteries and churchyards vary slightly on this, as it mainly depends on ground conditions. In Newark, at least, the water table was low, and so all double graves could be dug at 6ft 6in. In my early days this depth was insisted on, though as time went by six feet became the norm. The approximate depth of a coffin was 18 inches. When buried in a 6ft 6in grave, this left a depth of five feet for the second interment. On reopening the grave, you would then dig to 4ft 6in, leaving six inches between the two. Again, allowing 18 inches for the coffin meant that from the lid of the second interment to the surface was three feet. This was seen as an acceptable depth, as anything else could in theory attract the attention of certain animals such as dogs or foxes. Even burrowing animals, like badgers and rabbits, could in theory cause a problem. However, I doubt very much that this would ever happen. Do not underdig the grave. That's what I say.

Learning how to find the precise position of any grave by using both the pre-issued plot number and letter was a challenge in itself. It was as if each grave had its own postcode. However, finding them was not as easy as it sounds, and even today it occasionally catches me out.

Walking up the main drive from the London Road entrance, to the left is the east side (unconsecrated) and to the right is the west (consecrated). Both the plot numbers and row letters are the same on both sides; you just had to make sure that any graves you were going to dig were either on the east or west. (Always check your paperwork.)

Ted continued with his step-by-step guide, pointing out that all Christian burials were dug east/west. He then showed me how to mark out and cut the shape and set up the dig. When digging, he stressed the importance of adding on a bare minimum of four inches to both the length and breadth of any pregiven size. This allowed for clearance. 'You do not want to get the coffin stuck,' he said. Finally, he stated that I should always remove at least eight wheelbarrows of spoil from a new double, while only four from a single or reopened grave. However, this really depends on what type of spoil you're dealing with, but it's a rough guide. There was quite a lot to take in, and this did not include digging ashes, dressing the grave, backfilling, etc. Still it was more than enough to be getting on with for now!

I have fond memories of Ted Sumner. Besides teaching me all I know, he was the unofficial foreman that everyone looked up to on a daily basis. He sorted out the daily running of the cemetery. Even now, I can still picture Ted sat in the corner of the old donkey stable quite happily chuffing away on his pipe. The acrid smell of stale tobacco would whirl around that shed creating a thick, hazy, blue fog. It was awful, though at the time I never complained—I didn't dare. Your only escape was to stand outside, but on a cold winter's day it was not an option you willingly chose. Back then you just grinned and bore it.

If you ever dug out with Ted, it was always advisable to keep one eye on what you were doing and another on his pipe bowl. Ted would often lean over the edge of the dig, and if you were unlucky enough to be underneath, then hot tobacco would spill from his pipe and either end up on your head or, worse still, down the neck of your shirt. The man was lethal. If you dared to utter a word of complaint, he would simply unscrew the pipe's mouthpiece and flick the nasty, foul-smelling spit that he collected in the end at you. It was horrible! This is what earned him the name "Popeye".

CHAPTER 4

Initiation

While sitting out a summer storm, my new colleagues did their best to scare me with their own gruesome gravedigging tales. It was all in jest; however, I could only sit and listen as they asked themselves such things as, 'What if the lid of the coffin below suddenly collapsed, causing me to fall through it? Would I jump out? Would I refuse to finish the job? Or would the sickening smell of a decaying corpse have me heaving behind the nearest tree?'

Well, despite their valiant attempts to scare me off, their impressive stories, however true, did little more than intrigue me further. I would be lying if I did not admit that to some extent their gory tales had at least made me think. I was, after all, about to dig my first reopen grave, and yes, I was unsure of just what to expect. Still, I was not going to tell them that, was I? Especially as one work colleague had stated that I would not last three months. With that in mind, I was aware that my ability to dig, and so do the job, would be put to the test at the earliest opportunity. I wasn't about to give in.

Again it was Ted who showed me how to start and set up the dig before simply leaving me to get on with it. His only advice being that I was to 'continue digging until I located the coffin below', at which point I was to level off and measure up. Oh, and I was to 'keep my wits about me and watch out for a collapse'. With that I was simply left on my own.

In reality, despite their stories, it all turned out to be an anti-climax. The coffin lid held firm, there was no collapse (my only worry) and the digging was soft and easy-going (no complaint there). To be honest, I was relieved that the whole procedure had passed without incident—well, almost. No, the coffin did not get stuck, nor did it collapse! I had just finished and was double-checking the size when suddenly, creeping up and appearing from nowhere, came one of my colleagues who, with great amusement, shouted 'Gotcha' at the top of his voice. I nearly jumped out of my skin as he half scared me to death. My heart definitely missed a beat. I swore blind that I'd repay him for that, though I never did.

Well, I had now completed my first solo reopen dig. Although it had taken me nearly all day, I was really pleased with myself, though I was aware that it would take me more than one dig to convince my fellow colleagues. That would take time and a few more digs!

CHAPTER 5

Moonlighting

In truth I was still relatively new to the job, but when asked by a local undertaker if I'd dig for them outside my normal working hours, I immediately said yes. It was an opportunity that didn't come around too often; I just couldn't say no. It not only gave me the chance to earn a bit of extra cash, but it enabled me to try my hand at digging out in other churchyards. This in itself was a challenge! From water-filled graves to digging in the dark, and from solid clay to soft collapsing sand, some were easy and some were hard. It was an experience to say the least, and in some ways a welcome break from the norm.

Digging conditions varied from village to village. Most digs were straightforward and easy-going, so problem free. However, there were troublesome areas. Heavy, sticky clay, water and, of course, collapse often tried my patience. To be fair, digging in Newark was easy compared to places like Claypole, Beckingham, Long Bennington and Coddington. These, especially through the summer months, were tough going.

It was a brief venture that would end just as quickly as it had begun. From August 1982 until September 1983 I dug a total of 26 graves. In the process I was to visit 12 different churchyards, digging out most graves in the dark.

Most of the digs I dug with my brother Dave. On many occasions he was my "torch man". He'd often stand in the freezing cold shining a light so I could see what I was doing (those were the days). Later digs I was to complete with a fellow work colleague.

One of the most bizarre digs I was to do was a new double in a place called Averham. The grave was in a quiet little churchyard and was situated right beside a path. On the other side of the path, a mere three feet away, was the church's original "Black Death" plague pit. I only later found this out while talking to the vicar. Scary!

Possibly, though, the eeriest of all the digs I did was in Kelham churchyard. Believe it or not, it was the day before Halloween 1982. Picture this—I was in the middle of nowhere, digging out a single-depth grave. It was still, somewhat misty, with not a rustle of a breeze and total darkness (the "can't see your hand in front of your face" type of darkness). It was a strange place, especially in the dark; a bit spooky too. I was glad that it was a soft dig, and so I did not have to hang about.

Digging in the dark with nothing but a flashlight to guide you was certainly an experience. As most digs were over the winter months and straight after work, I was to do a lot of this. It wasn't an easy procedure, but once you'd cut the shape and got the size you wanted, you'd be surprised what you could achieve.

Locating the plot to be dug, especially when you're in an unfamiliar churchyard and with daylight fading fast, was sometimes fun in itself. Usually, the grave would be premarked by way of a wooden peg, which usually bore the deceased's name.

I recall a trip out to Morton to dig a reopener. That afternoon it had snowed heavily, and once I was in the churchyard, I could not find the wooden marker. I looked all over but could find nothing. Time was ticking, and I was beginning to panic; then suddenly I saw it poking out the top of the snow.

All Christian burials face east or west, but in many churchyards and cemeteries alike, not all headstones mark the head. To locate which way a grave faces, I was told a simple rule: as all churches are built facing east/west, it was simple—"head spire, feet altar".

It was after digging out at Claypole, on 8 September 1983, that everything came to a sudden halt. As usual the grave had filled with water. On the morning of the funeral the undertaker phoned Newark Cemetery and asked if my colleague and I could go and both dress and bale out the grave. The request was granted, and so off we went, thinking no more of it. On our return, we were to learn that news of our brief trip had been reported back to HQ (the town hall). Although the matter was never openly discussed with us, it did, in effect, bring our sideline to an end. From that day on I was never asked to dig outside of the Newark Cemetery gates again. It was a shame; still, it was good while it lasted.

CHAPTER 6

Phantom Digs

There's nothing worse than toiling away for hours and finishing a dig, only to be told, 'Sorry, lads, it's not going to be used. The family have changed their minds and would like it elsewhere.'

It does happen! I recall I had only been in the job a few weeks when a couple of my colleagues dug and completed a new six-foot double. It was in the old section, directly opposite the chapel doors. The following day the family had decided they wanted the grave to be in the new section. The already-dug grave was backfilled and never used and another was dug. My colleagues were not happy. I also dug and finished a six-foot dig, only to be told, 'Sorry, wrong cemetery. The grave should have been dug some 20 miles away.' Luckily for me, the grave could be left open and so used at a later date.

Another time saw a colleague half complete a dig before being told to stop. Apparently, the family had changed their minds and opted for a cremation instead. As I recall, this dig remained open for some 10 months.

It was then regarded as a "health and safety" hazard, and so it was backfilled. And yes, you've guessed it, two weeks later it was to be redug.

I can only recall one time when on the day of the funeral it was cancelled. It was a new double; the funeral was put on hold because on the eve of burying her husband, the wife too had died. A double funeral. It's not often you see one of these.

From time to time we all have bouts of forgetfulness. I once dug and dressed a grave and waited, but the funeral never arrived. As time ticked by, I checked with my boss, who told me, 'You idiot! It's tomorrow, not today.' Oh well; no harm done. Thankfully, incidents like these do not happen often.

CHAPTER 7

The Notorious Mr X

For a short time I once worked alongside a man who turned out to be a murderer. Who'd have thought it? I don't really remember too much about him. He was quiet, some might say a bit odd, but in general he just seemed an ordinary man who kept himself to himself. He joined as a summer temp and only worked with us for a few months before taking a job cleaning and maintaining the town's public conveniences. However, he left his mark! As a team we had always deemed each other trustworthy. The mess room was never locked, as there seemed to be no need. Then a spate of personal petty thefts led us all to question our integrity. It was small things that went missing, usually loose change or cigarettes. Nevertheless, it was damned annoying! We all had our suspicions but, as usual, no proof.

Then after one break-time a colleague and I decided we'd try to catch our opportunist thief. Our plan was simple, and although it was more like a childish prank, amazingly it had some effect. Hidden inside a jacket pocket, we discreetly left a small amount of loose change. Also hidden, primed and carefully positioned, was a simple mousetrap. Later, on our return, we found that the trap had been triggered and the bait removed. Although no one among us seemed to be nursing bruised fingers, the pilfering did stop. I guess our culprit had realized we were onto him. It was only after Mr X had departed that we were to learn that he had been sacked from his last job for, believe it or not stealing money.

It was not long before he moved on again and took a job as a school caretaker. It was while working there that he murdered a 13-year-old schoolgirl. In our mess room, on the day that we found out, there was total disbelief. It shocked us all. Unbelievable. In truth no one knew what to say; none of us could believe it.

During June 1988 my colleague and I dug out the young girl's grave. The funeral, as you would expect, was a very solemn affair for which the whole community had turned out. You could not fail to notice, never mind feel, the anger and pain felt by the silenced mourners. Only the cries of a grieving mother could be heard as her daughter's body was finally laid to rest. On the day, the atmosphere was potentially explosive as close family and friends vowed to seek revenge for one so young. 'A life for a life,' was quietly whispered.

Near on 10 years later I heard it rumoured that Mr X had been freed from prison. If true, then God help him if he was fool enough to return to Newark, for feelings still run high and vengeance is still sought.

CHAPTER 8

Machine Digging

If I had a pound for every time I've heard "By now I'd have thought you'd have a machine to do the digging", I could have long since retired. Truth is, for a short spell in Newark cemetery graves were machine dug, but never by me.

The introduction of a tractor-come-digger was all part of an up-to-date restructure. Older staff members welcomed its use with open arms, regarding it as a giant leap forward. I, on the other hand, did not share their enthusiasm. I remained sceptical, as I did not believe it necessary. Why was I so against it? I just believed that graves should be dug by hand—traditional skill that is usually passed on! I could have understood it if we were digging through rock, shale or heavy, sticky clay, but we weren't. In my eyes it just did not warrant it! Besides, machines often left a mess.

Over the years, I have spoken to many people about this, and it's surprising how many do share my view. However, I was outvoted, as my colleagues did not agree with me. It was only later, when the old boys

Ted and Walter retired and their manual positions were left unfilled, that alarm bells began to ring. When I questioned why, I was told that the machine could quite easily do the work of two and they weren't needed—it saved two wages. From five to three, job cuts, now we could see where they were really coming from. The real reason!

Our new machine? Well, after the briefest of demos, a fellow colleague stepped forward and used it for the first time, digging out a new double on the 3 July 1984. My usual digging partner soon adjusted to his new role, and for a time it did appear not only to save time, but to make life somewhat easier. This was until the first winter.

Firstly, the complex attaching of the hydraulic-digging arm proved a nightmare to fit, often taking three men to complete. It was frustrating and awkward. With no word of a lie, in the time it took to couple up the machine, I could be four feet deep digging manually. I kid you not, for I proved it.

What caused most concern, though, was that on average 6 out of every 10 new digs were collapsing while being dug. Newark's sand-and-gravel-based mixture was just too soft. The constant thumping of the digging arm against the thin adjoining walls was just too much; whole rows were falling into one, and as graves at this time were rarely shored, it became an annoying problem. This was only solved when we reverted back to digging by hand!

I lost count of just how many times teeth were snapped off the digging bucket. I also recall a time when hydraulic pipes blew, leaving the digging arm stuck in the grave. There was panic, as the dig was for that afternoon, and guess who was called in to finish it manually? I had to dig around the obstacle while the boss frantically found someone to come in and repair it. It was a close call, but all went well in the end.

Another time, in the depths of winter, I remember Ted saying to one colleague, 'You're the machine operator. You can do the digging.' It was bitterly cold, and snowing, and to make things worse, the machine had no cab. Open to the elements, my colleague froze while we sat in a warm mess room. On his return, he walked in covered in snow. I recall that he couldn't speak, as his lips had turned blue and his moustache had frozen. He was not happy.

What became of the machine? Well, eventually the hydraulic arm was duly detached and was not used again. Both the tractor and the digger were sold in 1994 and replaced with a nippy little truck. New hydraulic shoring gear was purchased and a demolition hammer was promised. All that was needed now was more staff!

Chapter 9

Class C's

"Class C" type graves are always an interesting dig. In truth there is no way of telling just what you may find. These graves were originally classed as paupers' plots; they were paid for by the state and, in Newark at least, would contain up to four unrelated people. Some were dug up to nine feet deep.

Information on these old plots was often sparse and vague, as not all rang true. All names were logged, but the grave depth was always a bit "iffy". I would often be asked to probe them, but it told you little, as most coffins had collapsed with time. Some plots were not fully used and were often bought by people wanting to be buried in the cemetery's old section. It was actually quite rare to be asked to reopen one, but it did happen. Today was one of those times!

Too soft. It may sound daft, but this was not a good sign. From the off I was aware that the soil structure wasn't quite as it should be; something wasn't right. It was then that the centre of the grave simply opened up. An air pocket, this cave-like void, could only mean one thing: the lid of the coffin below had collapsed. This was not unusual—in fact, I expected it—though it was too near to the surface, and that concerned me slightly.

At a depth of just 30 inches I suddenly found myself to be actually standing inside the last coffin buried. This I confirmed for sure when I unwittingly unearthed a skull. This immediately prompted me to recheck the grave's position, just in case I had mistakenly opened the wrong one. To my relief I hadn't. It was correct. Oh dear! 'How could this be?' asked office staff, when one vacant space should have remained, or so they'd thought.

There was panic at the town hall. 'Now what?' they asked. The funeral director arrived to view the problem before going to inform the family. I could only wait as they discussed their somewhat limited options. While they panicked, I took time to look closer at our newly found friend. It was then that I noticed something odd. By now my curiosity had got the better of me. It was the hair on the skull that had caught my eye; it just did not look right. It was positioned slightly to one side, thus covering one eye socket. It was kind of freaky looking. On taking a closer look, I carefully scraped away the surrounding soil. It was then that the whole hairpiece simply fell off. It was a wig; a curly, black wig! Needless to say, my colleague and I found it quite amusing.

Joking aside, it was now mid morning and the clock was ticking. There was no doubt that this prepurchased grave was full; so what now? On the funeral director's return, she duly told us what we had been expecting: we would have to dig a new single-depth grave. The challenge was set, and just to make it more interesting, the 1.30pm deadline remained.

So, with our backs to the wall and no time to waste, we hastily got stuck in. It was a close call, but we duly rose to the challenge and managed to fully complete the dig with a little time to spare. I guess the somewhat easy dig ensured completion, but it was a close shave! While my colleague and I toiled with this, another colleague had backfilled and put right the other dig. All were happy. This had been a typical "Class C cock-up". Still, it had made for an interesting morning.

The family had originally purchased two old "Class C" plots not too far apart from each other. Both had been used by the family just the once. One originally had room for two burials and the other just the one. I still believe that the details of the burials had been recorded wrongly. I think that although records showed that the plot we had dug had one remaining space, it was in fact now full. It should have been the other plot that we had reopened. Someone had got the plot numbers mixed up.

Chapter 10

A Practical Joke

A colleague and I once found a mannequin dummy that had been dumped in the cemetery. For a laugh, we removed the head and both arms, then near to the main drive in full view of anyone passing we buried the parts, thus making it look like someone was rising from their grave. From a distance we saw that it had the required effect!

Unfortunately, one old lady, who was visiting her husband's grave, saw it. It frightened her so much that she went running to the cemetery superintendent's office. He, in turn, immediately went have a look. He removed the plastic parts and apologised to the little old lady before returning to give us all a verbal telling off. No one could keep a straight face; even he had to admit he was amused.

CHAPTER 11

Restless Spirit

The east side of Newark's cemetery chapel (that's the left-hand side if you're walking up the main drive from London Road) was once used as a morgue after the bombing of the Ransome & Marles ball bearing factory (on 7 March 1941). Many died that day, including a woman whose body was never found. It is said that most of the casualties were taken to Newark Hospital. However, I was told that some of the dead were placed in Newark's cemetery chapel, where they remained until their burial.

On a rainy day in 1982 I was set the task of tidying up the chapel. On putting stuff away, I came across a chest of drawers. Inside I found, still neatly folded, a stack of white cotton sheets, as well as a vast number of body identification tags. This confirmed that the old-timers' story was indeed true.

The corner area that was used as the morgue was at that time doubling as our mess room. Workmen from the Commonwealth War Graves Commission would often work late and sleep over, staying in the mess room.

They often commented on hearing strange noises, whispers, and to feeling an eerie, cold presence. To be honest, although they swore blind that the chapel was haunted, it was always laughed off.

However, as the years progressed, a few mysterious and unexplained events did occur. I recall one break-time when, sitting with two other colleagues, the radio cassette we were listening to suddenly switched itself into record mode. It was very odd; both the record and play buttons were pushed down. Unfortunately, there was no cassette in it. I also remember when a green tennis ball suddenly, and without any help from anyone, rolled itself out of an adjoining storeroom and across the mess room floor. We cut our tea break short that day.

This was not all. After finishing a late shift, a road sweeper driver returned to wash down his machine. While doing so, he suddenly noticed a drop in water pressure. Believing that the hosepipe has simply become disconnected, he entered the chapel in order to refix it. It was then that he discovered that the pipe was still connected but the tap itself had been turned off. His immediate thought was that children were hiding, playing a joke, but it was dark and there was no one around. Besides, anyone entering the chapel would have had to pass him directly, and no one had! As you can imagine, he did not hang around.

So, could the east side of the cemetery chapel possibly be haunted? Who knows? Just maybe the spirit of one of those unfortunate victims still remains. These days the chapel is a storeroom and is blocked off from everyday use. To my knowledge there have been no further happenings. The graves of six of the bomb victims can be found just in front of the Polish war section.

CHAPTER 12

When the Coffin Gets Stuck

Without any doubt, the most embarrassing situation you can face as a gravedigger is for you to underdig the grave. I can recall just four occasions when the coffin got stuck. Only once was I involved.

It was the moment that I'd always dreaded and hoped would never happen. Seeing an enraged undertaker marching towards me before announcing quite bluntly, 'The coffin will not go in. Can you please come and sort it?', my heart sank. As I reached the graveside, the mourners had all but left. On viewing the grave, I was surprised to find that the coffin had in fact been interred. This seemed odd! So what was all the fuss about? In my mind, I knew for sure that I had allowed enough clearance, but on first glance it did appear to be an extremely tight fit. Something did not add up.

Curiosity had now got the better of me. Witnessed by a senior colleague, I duly climbed down into the grave, and while standing on the coffin, I proceeded to measure both its length and breadth. In truth I had to know just who was at fault. Happily, I could announce a "not guilty" from my side. I breathed a sigh of relief as I revealed the coffin to be some five inches longer than the actual size given. This was certainly one in the eye for this newly established funeral business.

A phone call of complaint was met with an apology from the director. I had been given the wrong size. I then learned that the size I had been given had not taken into account the coffin's lid, as it had been measured without it. Nor had they told me of the sticking-out handles on each end. The new-to-the-game undertaker admitted a "teething cock-up" and even came to see me. He apologised for his outburst and duly thanked me. News of the incident spread like wildfire. One local funeral director lost faith in us altogether; so much so that for each dig, they supplied me with a digging template. This I found insulting.

A simple communication breakdown was at the heart of another mishap, when a coffin had become lodged in a grave some 18 inches from the bottom. I had not dug it, but unfortunately I somehow found myself being roped in to sort it out. In front of mourners I was left standing precariously on top of the coffin while trying to scrape soil off each side, in order to slide the coffin down. This I did eventually achieve, much to my relief, though it was far from an easy task. It would have been much easier to have removed the coffin, carry out the work and then simply re-inter it. However, in theory the law does not allow this, and as a result I was left to save face and spare the blushes of my colleagues. Thanks, lads!

It was a similar story the first time I witnessed a coffin fail to fit its grave. I recall that it was left propped up in one corner while the problem was dealt with. What I found totally amusing was the heated argument that erupted. Superintendent Tommy Tate and fellow colleague Ted Sumner, who'd dug it, stood face to face and gave each other a tongue lashing as they both blamed each other for a mix up regarding the measurements. It was so funny, yet at the same time a swift reminder of what can go wrong.

It's not always the fault of the digger. Nevertheless, experience has taught me to play it safe and check and recheck everything in order to avoid these embarrassing situations. Believe me, it pays.

Chapter 13

The Old Gravedigger's Cottage

On what was once known as Sparrow Lane (now Elm Avenue) there stands an old cottage. This stone-built dwelling, once home to the resident sexton and his family, at one time had a well in the garden. I was once told that one of the sexton's own children had fallen into this well and as a result had drowned. I can't be sure of just how true this story is! However, in one corner of the garden there can still be found a thickly laid slab of concrete. This is believed to be the site of the old well.

As if one tragic tale is not enough, there is a second that befalls this secluded cottage. On Christmas Eve, 1966, the 15-year-old son of the last resident gravedigger was knocked from his bike and killed on his way home from school. His grave can be found not too far from where his home once was.

The cottage may well have hidden its tragic past, but not once had I heard it mentioned that the place was haunted. In 1994 a new family took up residence, and all this would change. Claims of ghostly goings-on were rife as the new occupants made it known that their dream home was indeed haunted. Ghost stories are debatable, but who'd have thought it? From page three of *The Sun* newspaper to an appearance on both local and national TV, their story just ran and ran.

It is said that ghosts do not like change! So could it have been the much needed renovation work that had initially sparked off events or was it just the family's overactive imagination? Who knows? They said their ghostly guest did not frighten them, nor were they at any time planning to move out because of it. To the contrary, this they said was their "little piece of paradise—their own bit of heaven", and they were quite happy to share. Oddly enough, once the story had died (so to speak), they moved out.

Everyone enjoys a ghostly tale, and I for one would like nothing more than to believe that the ghost of a child does indeed haunt the cottage. However, the fact remains that no other occupants have ever mentioned the presence of a ghost. To this day I've not heard further mention of it. What a shame.

CHAPTER 14

There's Always One

Although gravedigging would take up most of my working week, there were many other cemetery-related jobs that needed to be done—the most tedious of which was grass-cutting.

Personally, I always enjoyed mowing. A new season, out in the sunshine and fresh air, and of course there was always the chance of a free tan. You couldn't beat it. However, grass-cutting was not always a pleasure to do. Every so often there'd be a wet season when the grass would grow quicker than you could cut it. I have seen it as high as the headstones. It does lower morale, but priority was always given to gravedigging, and as a result grass-cutting was often neglected.

I have been moaned at it for it being too short, too long, too brown, too many daisies, too many dandelions and even for it being the wrong shade of green. Honestly, there were times when you could just not win. On a plus note, it wasn't all front-page news and letters of complaint; there were light-hearted moments and many amusing incidents, a few of which spring to mind here.

In my early days, for one day a week we'd be receive additional help from a colleague from the town's litter department. One morning, while mowing a particular area, my colleague was so eager to impress us that he duly outshone us all by carefully striping the entire area he was cutting. What was amusing was that he genuinely believed that in order to do this you had to first cut a breed, then miss a breed, mow a breed, and so on. Talk about laugh, we were in stitches for weeks.

At one point in time our main piece of kit for cutting grass was a large flail mower. It was lovingly, nicknamed "The Beast" due to the fact that it would eat up and spit out anything that crossed its path. It was an awesome machine but a truly reliable workhorse. One morning a colleague of mine was asked to change all of the machine's 32 individual blades. This somewhat tedious chore took him most of the morning. Unfortunately, without thinking, he removed all of the machine's blades before putting the new ones on. After carefully refitting all the new blades, he then proceeded to try out the machine, only to discover that he had, in fact, put them all on back to front. He was not amused!

Playing tricks on summer temps always brought a smile, especially when it was a naïve school leaver. I remember one lad asking a colleague, 'How do you start the mower?', to which he replied, 'Well, you need to bump start this one. What you have to do is run as fast as you can up the drive, and once you've reached full speed, pull the pull cord.' Well, this is exactly what this lad did, though after about 20 minutes of trying, he gave up and duly brought the machine back. He remained totally oblivious and duly announced, 'It won't start.'

On the same lines, a trick was played on me. My colleagues, without my knowledge, would, on finding my mower unattended, remove the spark plug cap. It always took a few minutes and a few beatings of the machine before I eventually put two and two together. Duh!

Finally, one old-timer had spent a summer's afternoon quite happily strimming grass. At the end of shift he packed away his equipment before coming over to chat with me. It was at this point that I noticed that the left lens in his glasses was missing. He, on the other hand, had not even noticed that he'd lost it. Unbelievable! It was like looking for a needle in a haystack, but nevertheless a colleague and I carefully retraced his steps, and believe it or not we found it. How lucky was that?

Chapter 15

A Strange Occurrence

Until it happened, I never really gave much thought to digging out a grave for somebody that I knew, a close friend, someone I had worked with or someone I occasionally shared a beer with. It's something you just don't think about, never mind expect.

Shivers ran down my spine on hearing the tragic news that an ex-work colleague had been killed. In truth none of us could quite believe it. He was a good friend and only young. He and I had shared a lot of laughs along the way. I had fond memories. It may sound morbid to some but it was an honour to be asked to dig his grave. It is the last thing you can do for anyone, and it meant a lot.

His grave was a new single which I had dug out two days prior to the funeral. On the day, and only an hour before they were due to arrive, it had been both checked, dressed and made ready. All was well! As the hearse pulled up and the mourners gathered, the worst thing that could possibly happen occurred! The grave collapsed. Immediately, I was called over by the undertaker, and on my arrival I was to find that the neighbouring grave had slid in and half filled the other. I could not believe it. Total panic.

As the family stood back, I began to clear out the grave. It was to prove a difficult task, as the spoil just continued to slide in. In truth, all that divided the two graves was a huge chunk of turf which just seemed to hang in mid air. I just hoped that it would stand for the duration. I had now done all that I could, and with that I redressed the grave and retreated. Luckily, there were no more hitches; the grave stood, and all else went as planned. What a relief.

Once the mourners had left, both the grass matting and the surrounding walkboards were removed. As I loaded up equipment and turned to fetch more, I noticed that my colleague was standing directly on top of that wedge of turf. It had obviously slipped his mind and before I, or anyone else, could warn him, he fell. He ended up face down, spread-eagled across the top of the coffin. Shocked, winded, red faced and extremely embarrassed, he quickly stood up, brushed himself down and promptly climbed out. He was somewhat dazed, as he had banged his head on the way down, though apart from that he was uninjured. In truth, he had been very lucky, as he had escaped any serious injury. To be honest, he could have fallen through the coffin; I dread to think of the outcome of that. If the grave had been a double, then who knows? It does not bear thinking about.

I'm pretty sure that, knowing this friend as I did, he would have thought this highly amusing. Talking to his brother, he too agreed, saying, 'I wouldn't be surprised if he himself had not orchestrated the whole event.' That, I would not have put past him.

Even now, it still seems odd that a grave could stand for two days and then collapse just as the family neared. I'm quite aware that you can never predict a collapse, but for a new single this is unusual. It was strange— very, very strange.

As for the well-being of my colleague who had taken the tumble, well, he continued to have nightmares about the whole event for quite some time afterwards.

Chapter 16

Three Nuns

Each working morning, at around 8.30am, three ghostly nuns could be seen crossing the cemetery. The nuns, dressed in traditional wear, walked single file, one behind the other. They would enter the grounds via the gate beside the old gravedigger's cottage. They'd follow the path adjacent to Elm Avenue but would turn and walk through the Commonwealth War Graves before disappearing through the gate at the Bromely Avenue entrance. If you were lucky enough to pass them by, then they would in turn greet you with a simple, yet cheerful, 'Good morning'.

Ghosts! No, of course not. Indeed, these women were as real as you and me. They lived in a convent situated on Elm Avenue, and by day they helped out a nearby Catholic school.

So why the ghost thing? Well, for one young lad who was working as a summer temp, the sight of these nuns for whatever reason just frightened him to death. It sounds daft, but in all seriousness it genuinely unnerved him. It bothered him so much that whenever he saw them, he'd just stop whatever he was doing and stand dead still with his eyes tightly closed until they'd passed by. 'Have they gone yet?' he'd ask. Why it bothered him in this way, I'll never know.

Yes, of course we gave him plenty of stick over it, but undeterred he continued to swear blind that these three nuns were really ghosts. Well, I guess there's nothing stranger than folk! And no, he did not finish the summer season. Apparently, he found the job too spooky.

Chapter 17

Collapsed Graves

If you're ever in need of an adrenaline rush, then you could try clearing out a collapsed grave as the hearse is coming up the main drive. It gets the old heart pumping, I can tell you. Collapsed graves are a real pain. Thankfully, it's not often they cave in, but saying that, one slam of a car door and in it can go. True!

Nowadays we shore most digs, though this itself does not fully prevent a collapse. If it's going to go, then it will. You cannot stop it. All you can do is prevent the top four feet from falling in on you, thus giving some prevention for your back, head and shoulders. It also makes it safer for the bearers and attending mourners.

I've been at the bottom of a six-foot double when one side, both sides and even the spoil heap has slipped in. It's frightening! In all my years only once has spoil spilled in enough to cover me up to my waist. That was scary! It trapped me, and I couldn't move. I was lucky, as a colleague was able to help pull me out. Often you are given no prior notice, as it just goes. Mostly it's just the one side, usually between the shoulders and foot. Occasionally, the grave wall will crack; self-awareness or an observant colleague may spot this in time, thus giving you the chance to jump out and get clear. If there is no time, then I have always found that if you stand with your back flush against the head-end wall, you are usually okay! This, of course, is the last resort. The head and shoulders are your safest bet and the strongest point. I guess it's because of the tapered shape.

For the first 10 years I used no shoring at all. Nowadays I often wonder how I dared to go to 7ft 6in deep without it. In fact, the deepest I have ever dug was 8ft 6in! I'm not what you'd call a lucky person, but at times I have more than ridden my luck with digging and have gotten away with it.

Today shoring is virtually compulsory, though sometimes you do have to use a bit of common sense. Up to a point you can read the ground, and during the hot, dry summer months you can dig the odd few without it. Yet in winter it's a very different story; with heavy, wet ground it's wise to allow the extra time and use it. It pays.

I once had a West Indian funeral where the grave had collapsed big time. In fact, I was still clearing it out when they arrived. Tradition has it that the family backfill the grave themselves. To be honest, the collapse was so bad, that it was not safe for them to do so, and although my foreman pointed this out, stating, 'It will be best to let the staff finish the job', they declined, saying, 'No, we will do it.' What can you do?

My worry was that they would stand on the edge of the collapsed side and, as a result, someone would fall in or get injured. However, there was nothing we could do except stand back and hope all went well. Thankfully, it did.

Eighteen months later I was called upon to reopen the same grave. This time my colleague and I were better prepared, as we had new hydraulic shoring equipment. As we dug down, we managed to install two units, and although the dig was shallow, due to the previous collapse, the grave walls stood firm. On the day, we were told that once again the family wished to backfill the grave. That was fine. What now concerned me was that we would have to remove the shoring first. This meant having to interrupt their grieving and in front of all not only remove the shoring but stand on top of the coffin in order to do so. This was a task that neither of us relished. In fact, we tossed a coin—and yes, I lost.

The undertaker agreed that at a given point in the service he would give us a simple nod; this would be the sign for us to begin. My colleague and I were truly dreading this point, as it felt like a true invasion of privacy. Then it came. The nod was given and in we went. The large group of mourners just stood and stared. They looked puzzled as they closely watched our every move. All eyes were now on us. It was an awkward moment. I had decided at the last minute that I was not going to get in the grave and stand on the coffin; I did not think the family would like it. Instead I reached down and attached the lifting ropes from above. It was not easy; in fact, I over-reached and pulled a muscle at the top of my shoulder—it was so painful! Then as the first unit was lifted clear, the mourners suddenly burst into song. "Glory Glory Hallelujah" rang out. What a relief, as it quickly diverted the attention away from what we were doing. Wow, that hymn never sounded so good. With the second unit out, we quickly retreated to the sidelines, where we gladly watched them backfill.

This had been an experience that I hoped not to repeat in a hurry. I told my colleague 'Next time someone else can take a turn', to which he agreed. However, I was to eat my words, and the next time was not too long in coming.

This time we fixed the shoring as usual but had agreed with the undertaker that we would remove it just prior to their arrival. This we did, but at a huge cost. Yes, the grave collapsed, and as a result it had basically half filled itself in the process. It was a right mess. The more I threw out, the more slid in; it was a no-win situation. In the end I managed to level it off and it kind of settled itself. It went close to the wire, but thankfully it held just long enough for the funeral to take place. Phew! And with the coffin interred, they again backfilled it themselves.

These situations are a nightmare, and once again I pledged that next time someone else could have a go.

CHAPTER 18

Sikorski Goes Home

This morning I was up and at work by a very early 3.45am. I was excited because I was preparing to do a side to my job that I have never done, nor may do again: an exhumation!

My task for now was to find out whether this Polish wartime leader's grave was either a brick-built vault or just a plain, ordinary backfilled plot. Working in breaking daylight, my colleague and I began by removing the turf and topsoil from just one corner of the grave. At around two feet in depth we hit upon what appeared to be a concrete base. This, in fact, turned out to be concrete slabs, which indeed sealed a brick-built vault. At this point, so as not to disturb too much, we were asked to chisel just a small hole through. However, breaking through the vault's lid was not that easy, as we discovered that reinforced iron strips ran the full length and breadth of the underside. It had certainly been well constructed.

Eventually, we cracked it; between us we had made a hole just big enough to shine a light through. Now, for the first time in 50 years, we were able to view the inside of the vault. What did we find? Well, there was a noticeable damp, musty smell, but more importantly, the vault had remained airtight and so was dry. The main concern had been that we'd find the coffin standing in water. It wasn't, and that was a relief to all. In fact, the coffin looked solid and in good condition. On top you could see the remains of a cross-shaped wreath. It was also possible to quite clearly read the nameplate. Intriguing stuff!

For now, that was as far as we were to go. It was now a case of waiting for the Home Office to grant permission for the final removal. It was later announced that the date for the exhumation would be 13/14 September 1993.

Right from the beginning, my colleague and I were told that we would be directly involved with the night's proceedings. This was not the case; at the last minute the job was given to a Lincoln-based funeral director. I was livid—so annoyed. I cannot put into words just how I felt. I could not believe it. I felt cheated, as they had poached the job from under my nose. I was not happy. Regrettably, I wasn't even invited to attend, which I still would have liked to do. Maybe if I'd have pushed a bit harder and made my feelings known, I could have been there. However, I was so annoyed at not being asked, that regretfully I did not pursue it any further.

As I was not present, I can only describe the night's events as told to me by the cemetery foreman. For the duration, the cemetery was closed to the general public. A large marquee covered the site, while a lone policeman patrolled the area. It all began with the removal of the headstone and surrounding kerb set. Turf and soil were then removed, exposing in full the vault's well-sealed lid. One by one the slabs were lifted. Also removed was one side of the vault's wall; thus fully exposing the coffin.

Then, with the underside well supported, the coffin was lifted out of the grave. The lid was then removed. This revealed the coffin to be within a coffin; in fact, there were three coffins in all, one of which they found to be lead lined and sealed tight. This was the one that held Sikorski's body.

In this were his remains, which were still wrapped in a standard army issue blanket. As the body had to be formally identified, it was lifted from the coffin and placed into a body bag. The blanket was then carefully removed. His remains were in remarkably good condition, so much so that you could still make out all of his features. He was formally identified by nothing more than his wedding ring. With this the job was declared complete and his body taken away.

After a memorial service at Newark's parish church, his body was returned to Poland. There he was cremated and the ashes interred in a marble sarcophagus. On 17 November 1996 a marble memorial was unveiled at Newark Cemetery. It marked the precise spot where he had lain for 50 years.

General Wladyslaw Sikorski had been the Polish wartime leader. He had died in a plane crash just off Gibraltar in 1943. For years they had tried to return his body to his native Poland, and now at last that wish had been granted.

CHAPTER 19

A Lucky Escape For All

A cold February morning, with a penetrating ground frost to boot. It was freezing. I can just about hack the cold, as long as there's no wind blowing and the sun's shining through. White over, still and crisp; that's how I like it. However, that was not the case today. It was raw. There was no shelter, snow was forecast and my feet were like blocks of ice. It was a bleak old day.

Digging out in these conditions is not ideal. I can't work wearing a heavy, restrictive coat, as I can't bend, which puts added pressure on my back and shoulders. Yet, I dared not take it off for fear of getting cold or, worse still, neuralgia; either way I lost. You'd think I'd be hardened to it by now, and in some ways I am, though these days I am feeling it more and more. Maybe I'm getting old.

For once it seemed that I had timed it right, as my colleague and I had completed the dig for today in full before the weather had changed. It was a deep one—a new 7ft 6in treble. The grave was safely shored and had stood the night, but due to the long coffin size the shoring units now had to be removed.

The trouble was that the units had frozen solid, and no matter how we tried, they just would not budge. This was because my supervising officer had refused to supply me with enough hydraulic fluid and, as a result, the mixture had contained more water than fluid; hence, it had frozen. In the end we had been left with no option but to dig out the units and forcibly remove them. Not a good idea. Once done, we duly dressed the grave and headed back to the mess room for a warming brew.

Some 20 minutes before the funeral arrived, I checked to make sure that the grave was still standing. Thankfully it was, and the cortege arrived in the middle of a fierce snowstorm. I stood shivering, with my back flush against a tree, while my colleague took cover by crouching at the base of a headstone. There was no escape. 'Hurry up,' my colleague muttered. 'Get the coffin in the hole and go home.'

I shared his view, as we both yearned for the funeral to end. Thankfully, for once someone was listening, and the chilled mourners did not hang about. In the circumstances, who could have blamed them? But at the time, and unknown to us, it had not been the cold that had dispersed them. Waiting by the grave was a perished-looking undertaker. On my arrival, he explained that the neighbouring grave, on which the mourners had stood, had collapsed. This, in turn, had sent mourners tumbling to their knees as they slipped into the grave. It was only by sheer good fortune that no one had been seriously hurt.

The coffin had been interred but was at a depth of about 4ft. What now? Well, one option was to remove the coffin and redig the grave, as it was just not deep enough. However, this idea was quickly knocked on the head, as it was deemed unsafe and foolish; it just would not have held. There was also the real risk that a second collapse would expose the coffin in the neighbouring grave, and this I did not need. The logical thing to do was to leave well alone and just backfill it, and this is exactly what we did.

As the grave was initially for three, the family was offered another neighbouring double plot free of charge. It was of small consolation, but there was little else anyone could do.

A short time later I was to learn that the family was planning to take legal action over what had happened at the graveside. They were planning to sue for compensation for injuries received after slipping under the surrounding walk boards.

I guess it could have been much worse. With hindsight we could have used a different shoring method (i.e. butterfly screws and woods), as this would have been adequate. Having to forcibly remove the hydraulic units had been a significant factor here. All the extra hacking and chopping of the sides of the grave had weakened the entire area, so as the ground slowly thawed, it simply gave way.

In the end the family chose not to pursue the matter any further. It was a let-off indeed and I may say a lesson learned in the process.

CHAPTER 20

Ignoring the Obvious

Looking for vacant plots in the cemetery's old section was like looking for a needle in a haystack. There were a few, but finding them was near impossible. It may look as if there is a lot of open, unused space, but in truth, all that ground is full. In many cases these graves are registered "Class C's" (unmarked paupers' graves). There are hundreds of them, and in many cases are those of children. However, from time to time I would still receive a request for a new grave to be dug in the old section. Each time, my answer was the same: 'Yes, I can check a few plots, but I can't guarantee anything. You're better off telling the family no.'

Well, despite my reply, I was on this occasion still asked to check the depth of a certain "Class C" grave. Records showed that it had been dug at 7ft 6in deep and that it had just been used the once. This in theory allowed for two more burials.

When checking grave depths, we used a six-foot steel probe. We nicknamed ours "Rodney". It was like a giant vampire stake. This probe was inserted into the ground and slowly pushed down until it located the lid of the last coffin interred, thus giving you a depth reading. The problem with this was that in old ground you could never get an accurate reading. More often or not the steel probe would go straight through the coffin lid, thus telling you nothing at all.

As expected I found nothing! The coffin must have long since collapsed. Only by digging the plot would I know for sure. From here on it was all guesswork. The family were told just what to expect, but nevertheless they were keen to use this plot, as it was near to other family graves. In fact, they insisted on using it.

It was a large coffin, needing extra width and length. Indeed, it was going to be a tight dig in the small space available, leaving no room for shoring. On the day, and at only three feet deep, I uncovered, running along the wall of the dig, a fully intact coffin. This told me that the grave I was digging was slightly off centre. This was not unusual, as the old rows rarely ran true. It was not a problem, as I was able to work around it, though I was worried that the grave might collapse. If it did, then it could bring the coffin in with it.

A foot lower and the digging suddenly came to an abrupt halt. Between us we had found a skull and various other bones. 'I thought this grave had space for two more,' I commented to my colleague. It was deep enough for a single-depth grave, but to squeeze two in would be tight.

The undertaker was called, and he in turn explained the situation to the family. They understood the problem but remained insistent on having a double-depth grave. With this I was asked if I was willing to continue digging, thus removing any remains that I found along the way in order to reach a reasonable depth. Not a pleasant task, but the dig was over a hundred years old, so I agreed.

One by one the bones were unearthed and carefully removed. All the remains were placed into black bin liners. These were later reburied in the same grave after the funeral had taken place. It was some job; still, we did manage to get the grave to a reasonable depth, so everyone was happy.

"Class C" type graves are always very unpredictable. As the new millennium approached and the cemetery filled up, one option was to start again, and so rebury using existing graves in the cemetery's old section. I'm not sure just how popular this would have been. My colleagues were not at all happy with that thought. 'Too scary. I'm not removing old bones,' one said.

I myself hope that it never happens, as new headstones would spoil the cemetery's Victorian look. It would lose its gothic character, and that would be a shame. *No, leave well alone*, I say.

CHAPTER 21

The Man Who Was Buried Twice

This was an odd one. The deceased (a man) had, at his own request, been buried at sea. Although his coffin had been weighed down with concrete and he had been laid to rest some nine miles offshore, it had somehow become snagged in the nets of a fishing boat. As a result, the coffin had been brought back to the surface.

His body was duly recovered, then some nine months after his first burial he was to be interred again. This time they were taking no chances; the deceased was buried on dry land in a single-depth grave in Newark Cemetery. The funeral was a low-key affair. Just a hearse, four bearers and four family members were in attendance. There was just one solitary bouquet of flowers.

CHAPTER 22

Exhumation

This may sound a bit clichéd; however, picture the night: a glowing full moon, racing skies, a gale-force wind. It was just like a scene from one of those old black and white horror films. Without a word of a lie, it was the perfect setting for the job I was about to do.

My task at this late hour (at the request of the police) was to reopen the grave of two children who they believed might have been murdered. Were they poisoned? That's what they hoped to find out. An exhumation is a gruesome task. This was a first of its kind for me—a one off—and slightly different from the "Sikorski" job. My colleague was not too keen on the thought of doing it, but I, however, found it interesting.

At 1am, just prior to starting, we were taken to one side and duly briefed by the head of Scenes of Crimes. They explained the procedure: how they would take soil samples at specific depths, how they proposed to lift the two coffins and how the dig would be documented and duly filmed at each stage. We were then both asked how we felt about doing the job. We both agreed that we had no problems, and with that we were simply told, 'Take it slowly. Nothing must be missed. You may begin work when you're ready.'

An hour of waiting in the cold had frozen us half to death, although hot tea laced with whiskey had to a point hit the spot. At least now we could get stuck in, much to our relief. We removed the headstone and turf, and in no time at all had found the original grave cut. It was to be 7ft 6in deep.

The grave was one of the few that had originally been machine dug. This meant it was oversized, though it made fixing the shoring somewhat easier. The dig itself was a clay-sand-based mixture, ideal for a quick dig.

The first soil sample was taken at roughly 18 inches deep, with a second at three feet. With the shoring fixed and the first stage complete, I continued with the second stage: to find the first coffin. By now, my audience was noticeably increasing. Unfamiliar faces surrounded me, watching and scrutinizing my every move. It was very off-putting.

The tent that covered us was too small. There was little to no room to work in; there were too many people, and the overhanging spotlight dried up all the air. It was oppressive and not the best of working conditions. By 2.45am I'd found the first coffin. After exposing as much as I could, I was then asked to take time out while forensics took over. More samples were taken before they continued in greater detail.

Using a bucket and trowel, they carefully removed soil from around and underneath the small coffin. It was a lengthy process. Their objective was to remove just enough soil to be able to lift one end. They then planned to carefully slide a sheet of thick polythene under it. This would help support the underside and so help keep the coffin intact when lifted. Once this was achieved, it was all hands as the first coffin was slowly lifted up and out of the grave. A success; it had been lifted intact, and so all were pleased. So far so good.

After an early morning lunch break we were to crack on with the final stage of the dig. It was now the turn of my colleague. It was a task he did not really relish, but nevertheless he got stuck in, and in no time at all he had hit upon the second coffin. At this point, just as before, the same procedure was repeated.

Forensics had worried that the dig would turn wet, which would have made life difficult for all. They had been concerned that the coffin might collapse when lifted. However, they need not have worried, as the dig had remained dry throughout and easy-going. As a result the second coffin was lifted with ease.

A final depth check revealed the grave to be some 7ft 10in deep; someone had done a good job. With one last soil sample taken, the task was declared complete. Finally, we were both duly thanked for the quickness and professionalism with which we had carried out the work. It was a nice gesture.

By then it was 5.15am. Now all we had to do was backfill a large, empty hole. Tired and truly exhausted, my colleague and I then went home. Not to sleep, mind. I took a bath and had some breakfast before returning to work by 7.30am, when I began digging out a new six-foot double grave. It was going to be a long day.

A few weeks later I was told that we might be requested to dig up the garden of the mother of the two children. The police believed that the drugs she had used to poison her children had first been used on family pets. They were looking for a connection. As it was, nothing came of this, so I guess it never happened.

Fourteen months later the two children were re-interred in the same grave. It was a quiet affair. The first coffin was lowered, and while two of my colleagues covered it with spoil, a priest said prayers. Then the second coffin was lowered before all present observed a minute's silence. This simple graveside service ended with a tearful father reciting a self-penned poem. He now hoped that his two children could finally rest in peace. His wife was convicted of their murder.

CHAPTER 23

Unmarked Graves

I once told a friend that I had buried 130 people in one day. 'Get out of it. You're having me on. No one can dig that many graves,' he said, looking somewhat bemused. In truth, I wasn't fibbing though; I was winding him up. I had dug out two individual six-foot graves, and there were around 130 sets of human remains. The remains had come from the crypt of Newark's parish church. How they came to be there is not clear, though I'm told that many were found by workmen while carrying out repairs and ground maintenance.

A colleague and I dug out the two graves on 10 and 11 April 1995. Five weeks passed and on 17 May, at 5pm, the re-interment took place. Most of the remains were in cardboard boxes. Each of these was opened and their contents simply tipped into the two open graves. The bones must have been quite old, as many were in really poor condition. Many were just fragments and dust, though some were complete. To think that here before us were two half-filled graves of persons unknown. Just a pile of bones with no names. It was eerie.

A mass grave; it was a first. Once the task was completed, the parish priest ended the proceedings with a prayer followed by a minute's silence. The graves were then simply backfilled and left unmarked.

Two and a half years later I was to re-inter a further 17 sets of human remains. These had been unearthed in the town's Old Friary Grounds. They were believed to be 500 years old and were possibly the remains of monks.

They're burial took place on 18 February 1998, at 12.30pm. This time the boxes were stacked unopened in one 6ft-deep grave. Thereafter, the procedure was not unlike before, though this time two attending architects marked the spot with a stone pot. Both jobs were unique; something you don't do every day.

CHAPTER 24

We Do the Work;
They Take the Credit

Brick-built vaults do exist, but thankfully they are few and far between. In all my years I can recall only four being built in Newark Cemetery.

The biggest hole that I had to dig clocked in at a whopping 10 feet long by 5 feet wide and 6 feet deep. It was massive! I began work on this oversized pit on 12 May 1994. From the off we had problems of just how to shore such a big hole. In the end we settled on using woods and Acrow props, but it was far from ideal. Although adequate, it took forever to fix correctly; this, coupled with the fact that we had just one day's digging time before the builders arrived, meant that the pressure was on.

A mixture of solid red clay and hard compacted gravel certainly slowed the job down. Although my colleague and I gave it our best shot, we knew that there was no way we could meet our 9am deadline. The builders would just have to wait.

It was no easy feat, but we toiled away and had finished three quarters of the dig before they arrived. I thought we were doing all right; however, one impatient builder got itchy feet and stepped on our toes by taking charge. With that, they all quickly muscled in, and between them they completely took over our job, thus sending us to the sidelines. Surely they could have waited for us to finish?

It appeared not. It was only then that we sussed out why. It was obvious that they had prearranged to meet with the deceased's family. Unknown to them, the builders were giving the impression that they were not just building the vault, they were in fact digging the grave themselves. What a bleeding cheek!

As you can imagine the atmosphere between them and us became somewhat tense. Tit for tat may be, but they should not have taken over my job. This needless rift widened further when our boss finally stepped in, forcing them to withdraw and letting us finish what we had started. Good on him, as for once he'd backed me up; however, the builders did not take kindly to being told to back off.

The vault, like most vaults, was for a traveller. A costly job; no wonder the friendly builders were so keen to please. The construction was of standard design: a concrete base was laid, on which a double-skinned, six-foot-high wall surrounding each side was built. Ceramic tiles covered the entire bottom three feet of the inside. They were white in colour, though some had prints of horses' heads on. I later learned that these prints, all different, had been specially made.

Talk about "spin the job out"; these lads were rubbing their hands. From start to finish it took them six days—twice as long as normal. It was a farce! Whenever the family arrived, they were there to greet them and show them how the job was progressing. Then, as soon as they had gone, it was back to the van where they simply sat it out.

The final insult came after we had finished backfilling and laying the many wreaths. It was then that the son of the deceased suddenly returned. The builders, who were just hanging around, were quick to meet him. I watched as he openly thanked them for all their hard work before giving each of them a cash tip. It was a swift smack in the eye for us and didn't they know it. As they left, their smug grins said it all. I'll not forget that sneering wave goodbye. We had certainly been had.

It wasn't long before the vault was reopened. My job was fairly easy; all I had to do was remove 18 inches of soil and expose the sealed lid of the second chamber. This seal was then broken and the compartment was tiled. Again, they were white in colour, but unlike before, some had a basic red poppy print.

I'm not sure if the contractors were one and the same— I seem to think so—but what I do know is that they botched the job. On sealing the vault this left a three-inch gap down one side. How they managed it I'm not sure, but what I *do* know is that they stuffed the gap with thick polythene. In time I guessed it would leak water. I wonder what the family would say if they knew?

There was one other brick vault that always stuck in my mind. Planning to commit suicide, paying for your funeral in cash and leaving precise instructions of what you want may sound far-fetched, yet one man did just this. I was told that he simply went into the undertakers, told them what he wanted and duly paid in cash. He also arrived on the scene when I was busy digging out his grave. Very strange, especially as he tried to tip us for doing so.

It was a double plot for him and his wife. The finished vault was tiled a ghastly royal blue for him and pink for her. Once it was finished, the vault was sealed and left until the day he died. On his death, his solid oak casket arrived in a traditional horse-drawn hearse. It was a grand send-off. There must have been a great deal of hardship in his life to plan in great detail this type of event. It certainly makes you think.

One of my older colleagues once spoke of a vault in Newark which is accessible via some steps. It is supposed to be in the old part of the cemetery, near to the area of the old morgue. There are a couple of hefty stone memorials, but as yet I have not come across any entrance. Maybe it's now buried. One thing is for sure, it would be interesting to know just where it is, or indeed if it does actually exist.

CHAPTER 25

Stumped

As soon as I realized the whereabouts of this dig, I knew it wasn't going to be easy. It was a prepurchased plot next to an established flowering cherry tree. Well, that was just asking for trouble!

From the initial cutting of the shape to removing the turf, it was clear that this was going to be a slow dig. Tree roots, and plenty of them, were the problem. They crossed the dig from head to foot, and removing them was an arduous task. Most of them I could handle, but there were two that crossed at the foot end that had me truly beat; they were just too big. One crossed directly at the foot, while the other, the bigger of the two, ran along the grave wall from the foot to just below the shoulder. Both were a good 10 inches in diameter. The work's small pruning saw was blunt and so of little use. This left me with no option but to concede and call in the lads from Parks and Gardens.

Two men brandishing chainsaws were quick to arrive, but they did not find it easy-going. I had dug around and under the roots in order to expose them, but spoil and small stones repeatedly jammed and blunted their blades. It proved a tricky, tedious, time-consuming task, but their perseverance paid off.

It was important to cut the roots so they would be flush to the sides of the grave walls. Luckily, the coffin was small, which made the job somewhat easier. However, it was still a tight dig, and with the job done, I thanked them for their help and simply continued to dig out. The remainder of the dig was pretty hard-going, as the tree roots had removed all the moisture.

I was so glad that I had decided to dig the grave the day before the funeral and not left it until the day; that would have been interesting.

Chapter 26

Blood, Sweat and Toil

The summer of 1995 was the hottest for 19 years.

August, another busy week, with four bookings and they were all six-foot doubles. The weathermen told us that the temperature was set to soar into the nineties. That was not ideal conditions for digging. With this in mind my colleague and I plumped for an early 6.30am start. It paid off, but as the sun quickly burnt off the cool morning mist, the heat soon blazed through.

In the summer it was not unusual for the ground to dry out. However, this year's intense heatwave had baked the ground solid; so much so that I was forced to pick the turf off. Digging was tediously slow going, and by mid morning it was, without a doubt, too hot.

Sweat poured from me as I toiled away at an extremely hard dig. The dry gravel crust was tough to break, and it proved just too much for my colleague. He blew his top. 'I really do hate this job. There must be more to life that this,' he moaned as he let fly with the pick. I just smiled, as I'd heard it all so many times before.

Day 1 – By 2pm it was unbearable. We had both had enough, so we decided to take time out under the shade of the trees. I had one of those thumping, dehydrated-induced headaches, and my colleague, through no fault of his own, had torn the skin from two of his knuckles. This was simply due to the fact that he whacked his fist, not once but twice, in exactly the same place against the burred edges of the shoring units. Ouch! Thankfully, it was the end of our shift.

Day 2 - As yesterday's dig had not quite gone to plan, I decided to pass one of the two remaining digs to two other colleagues. After finally finishing the one we had started yesterday, my colleague and I began another. As it happens both digs turned out to be tough-going, so it was a good call all round. Then disaster struck as between us we broke the only decent pick we had. My boss had played deaf to my plea for a new one, stating, 'Sorry, but they don't make them any more.' What rubbish. With that, he disappeared from sight and out of range of our whingeing. However, he returned a short time later clutching a bottle of orange and a bag of ice. All very nice, but it was of little help. A new pick—that's what I needed. But he refused to listen.

Today had been hotter than the previous day. It was heavy and humid, with not a sniff of a breeze. Very oppressive, these digs had taken it out of us all. The last few weeks I had dug some of the hardest graves I can remember. It was so dry, that the ground had baked solid. I was tired, I smelt, I was sunburnt and I was in need of a cool bath. Hooray for home time!

Day 3 – Today we had three of the four funerals. It's been a bit stressful, but we finished in time. However, I did have some concerns regarding the size of my other two colleagues' dig. It looked small and very narrow, I worried that it wouldn't fit.

The given coffin size was 6ft 7in long by 23 inches wide with casket handles. It was a big box. My colleague agreed with me, although he did not seem unduly concerned, but I would rather be safe than sorry. It was not my dig, and I should not therefore have interfered, as they would not thank me for it. Nevertheless, I had to say something; after all, if the coffin were to get stuck, it would have looked bad on us all.

Looking down into the grave, I could see that because it had been hard-going, my colleagues had let the side/ grave walls come in as they had dug down, so that the hole was wider at the top than at the bottom. I advised them to remove the shoring, as this would allow a bit of extra clearance; even then it still looked small.

Looks, however, can be deceiving, and on measuring it, it was indeed bigger than it appeared. They had not allowed as much clearance as I would have done, but it was adequate—just! It was just the casket handles that bothered me. They're chunky and sometimes they don't fold back down as they should. We wouldn't want to rip them off, would we?

Both my colleagues bore worried faces as the hearse arrived. As the coffin was lowered, I too held my breath. On passing me, it did appear to be a big coffin, but would it go in? I closed my eyes and only opened them on hearing my workmate whisper 'It's in.' Phew!

As the bearers had let the straps slide into the grave, I climbed down in order to retrieve them. Standing directly on top of the coffin, I could see how much of a tight squeeze it had been. There wasn't much clearance, but at least it had gone in. I guess that's all that mattered.

(That summer was so hot and dry that no grass was cut for 11 weeks—a record).

CHAPTER 27

Ashes? What Ashes?

Well, I guess it had to happen at least once. There's one rule when it comes to interring ashes, which is to give it priority. Make digging the hole your first job of the day or you're likely to forget them. Trust me. I know. So why did I fail to follow this all-important advice? I had been complacent and so did not check the paperwork—that's why. And as a result, I scored an extremely embarrassing own goal.

On what I thought was going to be a quiet afternoon, I began watering the newly planted flowerbeds. As I did so, I noticed that a group of people had begun to gather in the cemetery's car park. I thought nothing of it and continued with the task in hand. It was only when an undertaker arrived that I began to think, 'What's going on here then?'

I watched as he formerly greeted the waiting people. It was only then that the penny finally dropped. They must be here for an interment of ashes.

My worst fears were confirmed when the undertaker came over and quietly asked, 'Why has the hole not been dug?'

Totally stunned, I replied, 'As far as I was aware, there was nothing further booked in for the day.'

I could tell that he was not at all impressed with my somewhat lame answer. He just gave me a funny look and said, 'I think you'll find there is.'

It was only when I checked through my paperwork that I discovered, to my horror, that there was a booking and I'd forgotten it. For some silly unexplained reason, I'd somehow filed the interment details for the following week. It was totally my fault. *Well done, Ian*, I thought.

Now very red faced, I duly swallowed my pride and went over and apologised to both parties. My penance was then to endure digging out the plot in front of everyone. As if this wasn't bad enough, the plot in question was directly under a bush, and so was awkward to get at, never mind dig.

Yes, as you can imagine I found the whole incident extremely embarrassing. For weeks afterwards my gaffe became an in-house joke. I'd messed up and in true tradition my colleagues were not going to let me forget it. Hmm, the saying "he who laughs last laughs longest" springs to mind here. How very true; it would only be a matter of time before someone would beat this, and of course they did. However, I learned a valid lesson: don't forget ashes!

CHAPTER 28

Can You Dig Us Another?

To date, only twice have I been daft enough to dig out a grave in completely the wrong place. The first was a reopen grave. Basically, I forgot rule one: always check and recheck your plot number and read your instructions carefully. Hmm, sound advice.

For whatever reason, I didn't, and as a result I dug out on the east when it should have been on the west. Right number, right row—just the wrong section. Luckily, I realized around the halfway mark and so was able to put things right; and yes, I was the butt of all the jokes!

Before each dig we were always issued with burial instructions. This told you the name of the deceased, the plot number, the coffin size and the day, date and time of the funeral. Ted always said, 'Read, digest and hang onto that piece of paper, as mistakes do happen. It's the only proof you have.' He was right, of course.

The second time... Well, it wasn't my fault at all. While prechecking that a grave was dug, dressed and ready, a local undertaker was shocked to discover that it had been dug out in completely the wrong area. Puzzled, he duly checked with his office just in case he had given us the wrong information.

He hadn't. He then contacted the town hall, and he was told, 'Oh, sorry. There has been a clerical error.' This in effect meant that I had been given the wrong details. This 4ft 6in single, which should have been dug on the Methodist section, had been dug on the Consecrated side.

By now, the phone was red hot. It was decision time. What now? 'It's too late to stop the funeral. Is there any chance you can dig another?" asked the funeral director. All I had was 80 minutes, but I agreed that I'd do my very best. It was a pretty ambitious challenge, but my colleague and I were quietly confident. We'd just have to dig like the wind.

Not for the first time, this is where health and safety got turned on its head. There was no time to mess around with shoring; it was either the old way or nothing. If I fixed shoring, I could not guarantee reaching the correct depth, but without I knew I would be close or thereabouts. However, digging without shoring was now a disciplinary matter; I could get the sack! With this in mind I duly telephoned my supervising officer, but he would not comment. He would not give me a straight yes or no answer either way, so I went ahead and dug without.

The dig was typical for Newark—fairly easy going— though it was a close call. In truth, I was dressing it as they arrived. All went well, and everyone was happy;

I even got a thank you from the undertaker. That's more than can be said for my employers. It seems that no one was available to comment. A technical computer glitch was to blame.

Maybe, these things do happen, but nevertheless an apology of sorts would have been appreciated. Just think; if the undertaker had not come to check, there would have been some red faces—mainly ours, as we would have been on the front line.

CHAPTER 29

An Unpleasant Smell

Whenever digging out a reopen grave, there is always a chance that the coffin below you will collapse. It can happen at any point during the dig, and many a time it has caught me out.

Usually, there is no warning, but occasionally a hole will appear, thus giving you some prior notice of just what's to come. Sometimes the spoil below you will just give way, causing you to suddenly drop from anywhere between a foot and 18 inches, which makes you jump!

On one occasion the above-mentioned happened to a colleague of mine. Unfortunately for him, instead of the dig being a dry one, he fell into a foul-smelling, stagnant pool of water. The smell was awful! As you'd expect, he quickly climbed out. The water had come up over his boots and into his socks, and the leg ends of his overalls were wet through. Yes, it was pure "vomit behind the headstone" material. Not pleasant. With that, my colleague immediately went home to get changed. He had to throw away his socks, boots and overalls. I can't say I was surprised.

Fortunately, although I've fallen through my fair share of coffins, I have so far been spared the above.

CHAPTER 30

All's Well That Ends Well

It's a noticeable fact that over the years people have become taller, broader and wider. As a result, grave and coffin sizes have become bigger. In Newark Cemetery the spaces allocated between plots and rows have not changed since the early 1980s, and this, with the addition of shoring, means that there is little to no dividing wall between each grave. These factors contribute to an increase in grave collapse and was the main factor regarding one particular grave I dug. This was a big one—a treble at 7ft 6in deep. From the start, it had "collapse" written all over it. I had shored it using woods with butterfly screw supports— this was an adequate safety shield—but the digging was too soft and sandy, and in truth I did not expect the dig to stand the night. In the morning the grave had collapsed, though the amount was small and not enough to concern me. The shoring had done its job, and with that I cleared it out, dressed it and made it ready for the funeral. I did one final inspection just 10 minutes before they arrived, and all was fine. I watched as the hearse arrived, closely followed by six black limos.

Less than 10 minutes later the phone rang. My heart immediately missed a beat. I answered, and the exact words I heard were, 'Oh, hello. There seems to be a problem with the funeral. The coffin won't go in the grave. Please can you go and sort it. Thank you.' With that, they hung up.

My head dropped and my heart sank. I took a deep breath before my colleague and I went off to face the wrath of the gypsy clan. Needless to say, the colleague I had originally dug out with had scarpered. I'd asked him to come with me, but he refused point blank, saying, 'It has nothing to do with me. I am not going near it.' Typical.

At the graveside I was relieved to find that it was just that the grave had collapsed; this was bad enough, but at least no one was to blame, as it was just "one of those things". My guess was that, as the grave was near to the main drive, the repetitive slamming of car doors had triggered the collapse. For safety reasons I just wanted to level out the excess spoil. However, the family insisted that I redig it out, back to full depth. I had little choice but to agree, and so with dozens of pairs of eyes watching my every move I began.

Throughout, the grave continued to collapse. I had two major concerns, the first being that this grave was deeper than the one next to it, thus the coffin in there could possibly slide over with the spoil. If this happened, I would have had a real problem. As it was, I could see the rim of the coffin lid and some of the coffin side, though I did not let on to those that were watching.

Instead I gently and discreetly patted the moist sand around any visible areas, hiding them from view. Secondly, I was concerned about the other side; if that collapsed... Well, it didn't bear thinking about. In all it took 30 minutes to put right. The funeral passed without further incident.

Health and safety states that I should not have entered the grave to do what I did. By rights the grave should have been abandoned, backfilled and another redug, all on the same day. This is easier said than done when you have a large number of graveside mourners. If I had asked them to come back later, they would have dug the grave themselves!

This grave still has to be reopened twice more. It's not a job that I'm looking forward to, as it will be anything but straightforward. Oh well. All's well that ends well.

CHAPTER 31

Arctic Conditions on New Year's Eve

It was New Year's Eve 1996, and I was digging out a new six-foot double grave. It was my 133rd dig of the year—my second busiest ever. Overnight it had snowed, and, wow, we'd had more than the norm, which was unusual for this area. It had certainly caught everyone out, including ourselves.

Our toilets, mess room and water supply had all frozen. 'What? No tea?' we shouted. That prospect was not good. Not to worry, as our survival techniques knew no bounds; we improvised and melted some snow.

My digging colleague was in a foul mood, as he hated the snow. He also made it quite clear that it was New Year's Eve, and he did not want to be at work. This was a view shared by us all, but unfortunately we had one grave to dig and another to backfill.

It took me quite some time to pluck up the courage to leave the warm mess room, but once out and about and the circulation got going, it wasn't too bad. The snow was deep and the wind was bitter, but despite a hard-penetrating ground frost, digging was quite easy going. My main concern was a huge, tall headstone which backed onto the foot end of the dig. It was leaning slightly but not loose; nevertheless, it gave me concern. If it happened to fall while I was digging, then... Well, it didn't bear thinking about. It was indeed a health and safety risk, though there was very little I could do about it. It was far too big for us all to manhandle and lay down, and we didn't have the equipment or the space needed to rope and secure it either. My health and safety officer was still on Christmas leave, so it was a case of taking a chance.

As it was, the area in which I was digging was renowned for being soft. The ground was indeed heavy and the grave walls were spongy. Our only plus was that the grave was well shored. Touch wood, it would stand over the next couple of nights.

With a collapse possible, I decided not to fully complete the dig. I basically reached the required six-foot depth but then closed it down, leaving both the measuring and shaping of the grave until my return on the 2 January 1997.

It was good timing too, as the day's only funeral was now due. It was then that the fun and games started. Despite repeated requests, which always fell on deaf ears, I had no road salt to spread on the cemetery's main drive. As a result, both the hearse and following cortège got stuck as they tried in vain to negotiate the slight incline around the base of the war memorial. Vehicles were sliding in all directions. For a time it was chaos.

For a moment it looked as if we'd have to give them all a push.

Thankfully, everyone managed to avoid hitting both the memorial and, indeed, any of the lime trees that lined the drive on both sides. It took a bit of doing, but at a snail's pace they all managed to get to the graveside in one piece.

The day had been bitterly cold. I didn't mind working in the snow. The wind, however, and the minus chill factor around my ears is something that I cannot bear; it drives me insane. I must say I was glad to get finished and get home, though I did pay for it later. My ears zinged, and I got cold in my neck and shoulders. Oh, the joys of being a gravedigger! Oh well. At least I found time to throw a few snowballs, and between us we even made a snowman.

CHAPTER 32

Peace of Mind

'No, no, no,' she shouted. 'I don't care what you say. That memorial tablet has been laid in the wrong place. My father is not buried there.'

Wow, was she feisty! She was blunt, direct and to the point, and she was not prepared to listen to anyone. She was adamant that I was wrong and she was right. No matter what I said, she still believed that the plaque covering the plot of ashes in the Garden of Remembrance had been fixed on the wrong plot. There could be no reasoning with her, as she just would not listen.

In order to clear up the matter, I checked both our interment plans and our booking diary. It all tallied, but she was having none of it. She would not believe me. In her eyes I had messed up. However, I knew that it was correct. She was so incensed, that she demanded an internal investigation.

As she stormed off, she vowed to have the plot reopened and the nameplate on the casket checked. I could do nothing; not when she was in that frame of mind. It was pointless trying! Besides, I didn't get paid to take verbal abuse. So I walked away.

Time did not heal this, and she would not let the matter drop. Eventually, her persistence paid off and it was agreed that the plot would be reopened. A date was duly set. It was also agreed that she should be present, to witness the outcome at first hand.

On the day, although I was present, I left it to the cemetery foreman to dig out and reveal all. There was total silence for the duration of the dig. Although I was 100 per cent certain of the final outcome, I did still have a brief moment of doubt. *Hmm, what if I was wrong? We'd be front-page news for sure.* I tried not to think of that outcome. Besides, it was right. I knew it was! I kept telling myself it was.

Finally, the moment of truth came. The foreman, now on his hands and knees, finally brushed away soil from the top of the casket and revealed the nameplate in full. He then read out loud the inscription, and the debate was settled once and for all. It was indeed the correct plot!

Maybe now the woman could rest easy in the knowledge that her loved one was safe. The woman herself never spoke, never thanked anyone and never apologised; she simply got on her bike and quietly rode off. But at least now her peace of mind was assured!

It was not long before I received a similar request, though this time the circumstances were slightly different. This woman had had her husband's ashes buried during a busy spell. I had interred three different sets of remains on the same row in the same week. On revisiting the plot, she had become confused as to which one was her husband's. Distraught by this, she asked if I could please check out the plot number. This I did, and unfortunately it revealed that she had actually been attending the wrong one.

Upset by this, she promptly applied to the Home Office in order to get a licence to exhume the ashes. The licence was duly granted, and once again a date was set. On the day, the plastic urn was correctly identified, and so removed, and the plot simply backfilled. What became of the ashes? Well, I was told they were reboxed and buried in her garden.

CHAPTER 33

Easily Spooked

Gravedigging is not for everyone. Many people on seeing me digging out have commented, 'Oh dear. I couldn't do your job. I'd never sleep at night.'

To be fair, you rarely see anything. Occasionally, you come across a few old bones, but that's about it. Compared to what an undertaker must see, gravedigging is by far the easy part. Nevertheless, there are very few people willing to give it a go.

One new boy on only his first dig stressed the point that he did not fancy digging out reopen graves. He was a big, strapping lad, but he openly admitted that it wasn't the digging he feared; it was the thought of falling through the lid of the coffin that put him off. In fact, it worried him so much that whenever I asked him to dig, his usual response was, 'Ask someone else to do it.'

As cemetery foreman, it was now my job to teach any newcomers the art of just how to dig a grave. Unfortunately, this colleague was not willing to learn. This was not the job for him, so why take it? I later learned that he had in fact taken the post under the illusion that he was too old to dig. He repeatedly stated that it was a young man's game.

While working with me on a six-foot reopen grave, he made it quite clear that he was not at all comfortable with the task in hand. So much so, he promptly announced, 'If the coffin lid collapses, you won't get me in another.'

The first two stages of the dig, reaching 4ft 6in in depth, he was okay with, though his mood was soon to change. While removing the head end of the dig, taking it to six feet in depth, I had not only unearthed a couple of coffin screws, but I had hit water. With all the wet weather we'd had, the water table had risen (unusual for Newark), and although a good six inches of spoil separated me from the coffin lid, it was still wet and smelly. Knowing this, he was quite reluctant to take his turn at digging. 'If you've thrown out two coffin screws, then the lid won't be solid,' he said as he gingerly climbed down the ladder into the grave.

'You'll be okay,' I replied, smiling to myself and willing the coffin to collapse under him, as he was a miserable old so-and-so and no fun to work with.

However, the coffin lid held firm—more's the pity! I watched as he stood with legs apart, both feet straddling the inner edges of the dig, while shovelling like the wind in order to get done. He threw soil just about everywhere, including back on himself, for which he kept giving me a dirty look, as he obviously thought I'd thrown it back in on him. He had no intention on spending any longer than necessary in the grave, and after about 20 resentful minutes he'd had enough and duly climbed out. 'What about levelling off and shaping up?' I asked. 'You've not finished yet.' He did not reply and just gave me yet another of his dirty looks.

'The more you do, the easier it becomes,' I commented, but again I got no response. With that, I took off my jacket and proceeded to complete the job myself; it was easier that way. Although my colleague stayed in the job, he was quick to distance himself from the digging side. As a result, he hardly dug any graves, especially reopeners.

In all my years only once have I witnessed a colleague fall through a coffin, which frightened him so much he declined to finish the job. He never dug another and left soon afterwards.

CHAPTER 34

Strange People

The Woman With the Yo-Yo Dog

Every Friday wind, rain or shine, this little old lady would come to the cemetery to attend the family grave. Beside her would always be her Jack Russell dog. Without a word of a lie, all this dog ever did was pogo up and down on the end of its lead as it walked beside her, barking. Woe betide anyone who approached or passed her by, as the dog would go for them, snarling as it did so. It was an extremely vicious little dog, though very protective of her. It must have driven her barmy. It did us.

MR Spirit Level

This man would visit the cemetery at least twice a week. Each time he came, he would bring with him a tape measure and a spirit level. He was obsessed. Firstly, he would check that the grave was level, and then he'd measure the height of the grass. If it exceeded in height, then out would come a pair of scissors, and with that he would give it a needed trim. Woe betide anyone who ran over the grass with a mower.

Pram Man

This man was very strange indeed. When he first started visiting, no one really took any notice; he was just an ordinary man pushing a pram! But, after three years or so, we realized that surely any child would be walking by now, and so why was he still pushing a pram? Over time his visits continued and our interest grew; so much so, that my colleague and I decided to try and sneak a look into the pram. In truth, it was no easy feat; in fact, it took us months to time it just right. More often than not he'd spot us coming and head off in the opposite direction. Then one day we met him head on, and I managed to peek inside. I could not believe it; it was a doll. Very odd. His pram was always gleaming clean, and on hot days it even had a parasol in order to keep the sun off. To this day he still occasionally visits.

Sock Man

For a short time this man was a regular visitor to the cemetery. He'd sit on a bench and remove both his shoes and socks before putting his socks back on, though on the opposite feet from which they came. He would then put on his shoes and walk off. Come the next bench, he would again sit down and repeat the same procedure. Occasionally, he would even produce a new pair from his pocket and do a complete swop. Oh well, as the old saying states, "There's nowt so queer as folk."

CHAPTER 35

Cemetery Wildlife

The last thing you would expect to find wandering freely around a cemetery would be a tortoise. Well, it happened. In the 1970s one did just this. When I was first told, I just laughed and humoured the old codgers. However, they swore blind that they often saw it during the summer months. They said that the tortoise's shell bore the scars of workmen with scythes. Nevertheless, it was resilient enough to survive for many years. No one recalled from where it came or indeed its fate. They presumed it must have perished during the cold winter months.

"Tree rats" or grey squirrels are fun to watch—incredibly agile, and destructive beyond all belief. Their actual numbers were always hard to define, but at their height I personally counted at least 13. At one point youths with air guns nearly killed them off, but they are natural survivors, and so they lived on.

In the summer, just like the crow, they would watch as someone placed fresh flowers on a grave. Fresh flowers meant fresh water, and they soon cottoned onto this.

Both parties would patiently wait, and once the path was clear they would make their move. One by one they would pull out all the flowers, tossing them aside in the process. Their prize was the fresh water. Until you have witnessed this event first hand you would not believe it. I have lost count of just how many times the cemetery staff have taken the blame. Still, life without the squirrel would not be the same.

In the spring they'd demolish the first wave of sweet-smelling crocuses as they searched for that hidden nectar, saffron. They would steal birds' eggs and uproot daffodil bulbs. They would stop at nothing, and there was abundance for them to go at. Come the autumn, they would gorge themselves silly on berries and nuts. They'd stash them and randomly bury them, yet they seemed to forget where they had hidden them.

If you were alert and watched them closely and were quick enough to pick up the signs, then it was possible to actually predict a sudden change in the weather. Before rain or snow you could find them busying themselves, feeding up before taking to their drays. They would only re-emerge when the storm had passed.

Catching and removing mice, or indeed rats, from the bottom of a six-foot grave is not easy. Mice, although not easy to catch, can usually be dealt with. Rats, however, are a different story. Facing a rat in such a confined space? No thanks! Thankfully, it does not happen too often. When faced with this situation, I'm afraid to say that the rat has to be killed, though I won't tell you just how we do it.

One animal we don't see too often these days is the hedgehog. There used to be many, but over the years the dense undergrowth has either been cut back or removed, and if you see one now you're quite lucky. I do recall a time when one had fallen into a grave and had buried itself into the side. It was only by sheer chance that I spotted it and so was able to free it.

Moles were once an annoying problem. For a time, they popped up everywhere. They were so difficult to shift, and although we tried to smoke them out, they always came back. Oddly, over time they moved on by themselves; it's now been a number of years since I've seen any trace of one. I'm told they do not like noise, so maybe the Gator truck we use keeps them away.

Grass snakes have often been seen slithering about, though they're usually quick to escape the wrath of the mower. We did once find a nest buried deep inside a leaf-mould heap. Today they can still be found, and if you're really lucky, you can sometimes find a complete shed skin.

I can just about tolerate bees, but I draw the line at wasps. I hate them. They are horrible things with one sole purpose in life, and that is to sting you. I can recall a time when a colleague was busy strimming grass, only to disturb a very large nest. They got under his visor and on his clothes. I have never seen a man run so fast. The foreman, a bunch of building contractors and I nearly died laughing as he ran past us, tearing off his clothes as he went. He received a standing ovation as he passed, though he was not happy.

In one respect he had been very lucky, as he had only been stung twice. However, both were on the back of his neck, and that was more than enough for anyone. Usually, when a nest was found, it was marked and dealt with accordingly. One old-timer once put a stone pot over the top of a nest opening, then for some daft reason he went back and removed it. They swarmed out and chased him; and yes, he got stung—ouch!

Foxes have lived in the cemetery for a number of years now. Their den is well hidden, and only a few people know of its whereabouts. The first known litter of young, we found dead just feet away from their home. A passer-by told us that he had seen a man with two terrier dogs hanging around the den's opening. Judging by the marks around the cubs' throats, it was obvious that the dogs must have killed them. The adults must have escaped, and for a time the den was not used. However, they did return, and as far as I know, they are still there.

There was at one time a wise old owl that lived in a skeleton of an oak tree. Its home had been nothing more than a hollowed out trunk that lay hidden in an overgrown part of the cemetery. I never saw it, though the old boys spoke of hearing its calls on a winter's afternoon.

The crow. What a clever bird this is. I like to hear the noise made by a murder of crows in the trees above; it gives the cemetery that gothic feel. They can be quite violent too. In times of hardship, when food is scarce, I have seen them take baby birds and chase squirrels and even cats. They're not afraid of much.

Over the years I have seen various other birds, animals and insects. They include ferrets, weasels, budgies, parrots, woodpeckers, frogs and toads, bats, ducks and even the odd bird of prey. The list is endless.

You'd be surprised what wildlife you can find in a cemetery. Why not walk down and take a look for yourself?

However, I can't finish without mentioning "dead man's flies". These annoying little flies, more commonly known as fruit flies, are about the third of the size of a meat fly. When digging, especially when doing smelly reopen digs, they truly drove you insane. From June to September they'd be under your arms, in your mouth, up your nose, in your ears and eyes and would constantly be buzzing around your head. They were a real pain!

Of course, they were not really "dead man's flies"; and no, they did not come from out of the grave. Still, just the thought of this was more than enough to put off many of my colleagues.

THE END

 CPSIA information can be obtained
at www.ICGtesting.com
Printed in the USA
LVHW030626020322
712306LV00002B/316